This Journal Belongs to:

:

Made in the USA
Monee, IL
09 February 2023

27423856R00056